I0439838

June 2014

NUCLEAR NONPROLIFERATION

Additional Actions Needed to Increase the Security of U.S. Industrial Radiological Sources

GAO
Highlights

Highlights of GAO-14-293, a report to congressional requesters

NUCLEAR NONPROLIFERATION

Additional Actions Needed to Increase the Security of U.S. Industrial Radiological Sources

Why GAO Did This Study

In 2012, GAO identified security weaknesses at U.S. medical facilities that use high-risk radiological sources, such as cesium-137. This report addresses potential security risks with such sources in the industrial sector. Radioactive material is typically sealed in a metal capsule called a sealed source. In the hands of a terrorist, this radioactive material could be used to construct a "dirty bomb." NRC is responsible for licensing and regulating the commercial use of radiological sources. NNSA provides voluntary security upgrades to facilities with such sources. GAO was asked to review the security of sources at industrial facilities. This report examines (1) the challenges in reducing security risks posed by industrial radiological sources and (2) the steps federal agencies are taking to improve security of the sources. GAO reviewed relevant laws, regulations, and guidance; interviewed federal agency and state officials; and visited 33 of about 1,400 U.S. industrial facilities selected based on, among other things, geographic location and type of device using the radiological source.

What GAO Recommends

GAO recommends, among other things, that NRC assess the T&R process to determine if it provides reasonable assurance against insider threats. In addition, GAO recommends that NNSA, NRC, and DHS review their collaboration mechanism for opportunities to enhance it, especially in the development of new technologies. NRC generally agreed with GAO's recommendations, and NNSA agreed with the one recommendation directed to it. DHS did not comment on the report.

View GAO-14-293. For more information, contact David C. Trimble at (202) 512-3841 or trimbled@gao.gov.

What GAO Found

GAO found that challenges exist in reducing the security risks faced by licensees using high-risk industrial radiological sources. Specifically, licensees face challenges in (1) securing mobile and stationary sources and (2) protecting against an insider threat. Regarding mobile sources, their portability makes them susceptible to theft or loss, as the size of some of these sources is small enough for them to be easily concealed. The most common mobile source is contained in a device called a radiography camera. GAO identified four incidents from 2006 to 2012 where such cameras that use high-risk sources to test pipeline welds were stolen. These thefts occurred even though the Nuclear Regulatory Commission (NRC) has established increased security controls. Licensees also face challenges in determining which employees are suitable for trustworthiness and reliability (T&R) certification to have unescorted access to high-risk radiological sources. GAO found two cases where employees were granted unescorted access, even though each had extensive criminal histories, and one had been convicted for terroristic threats, which include a range of violent threats. In this case, NRC said that the person was convicted not of a threat against the United States, but of making violent verbal threats against two individuals. It is unclear whether these cases represent isolated incidents or a systemic weakness in the T&R process established by NRC. Without an assessment of the process, NRC may not have reasonable assurance that access decisions made by licensees can prevent threats to high-risk radiological sources, particularly by a determined insider.

Federal agencies responsible for securing radiological sources—including NRC, the National Nuclear Security Administration (NNSA), and the Department of Homeland Security (DHS)—have taken steps to improve the security of industrial radiological sources. For example, NRC is developing a best practices guide that is expected to provide licensees with practical information about how to secure their sources. Also, NNSA is developing new technology that would, if successful, improve tracking of radiological sources while in transit. However, GAO found that although the agencies have been meeting quarterly to discuss, among other things, radiological security, this mechanism did not always help them collaborate and draw on each agency's expertise during research, development, and testing of a new technology for a mobile source tracking device. By not collaborating consistently, the agencies have missed opportunities to leverage resources and expertise in developing this new technology to track radiological sources. This technology could aid in the timely recovery of a lost or stolen radiological source and support the agencies' common mission. As GAO has previously reported, when responsibilities cut across more than one federal agency—as they do for securing industrial radiological sources—it is important for agencies to work collaboratively to deliver results more efficiently and in a way that is consistent with the federal government's multiple demands and limited resources.

Contents

Abbreviations

DHS	Department of Homeland Security
DOE	Department of Energy
DOT	Department of Transportation
FBI	Federal Bureau of Investigation
GPS	Global Positioning System
GTRI	Global Threat Reduction Initiative
IAEA	International Atomic Energy Agency
NNSA	National Nuclear Security Administration
NRC	Nuclear Regulatory Commission
NSTS	National Source Tracking System
PNNL	Pacific Northwest National Laboratory
T&R	trustworthiness and reliability
USDA	United States Department of Agriculture

June 6, 2014

The Honorable Thomas R. Carper
Chairman
The Honorable Tom Coburn, M.D.
Ranking Member
Committee on Homeland Security and Governmental Affairs
United States Senate

The Honorable Claire McCaskill
Chairman
Subcommittee on Financial and Contracting Oversight
Committee on Homeland Security and Governmental Affairs
United States Senate

The Honorable Robert P. Casey, Jr.
United States Senate

Radioactive material is used worldwide for legitimate commercial
purposes, including industrial processes in the oil and gas, aerospace,
and food sterilization sectors. Material used for these purposes is typically
sealed in a metal capsule, such as stainless steel, titanium, or platinum,
to prevent its dispersal and is commonly called a sealed source.[1] Some of
these sources are highly radioactive and are found in a wide variety of
devices, ranging from mobile industrial radiography sources containing
hundreds of curies of iridium-192 to larger irradiators with thousands, or
even millions, of curies of cobalt-60.[2] The facilities where these sources
are contained include, among other things, warehouses, commercial
facilities, and research buildings.

In the hands of terrorists, these sources could be used to produce a
simple and crude, but potentially dangerous weapon, known as a
radiological dispersal device or dirty bomb, whereby conventional

---

[1]Such material includes americium-241, cesium-137, cobalt-60, and iridium-192.

[2]A curie is a unit of measurement of radioactivity. In modern nuclear physics, it is precisely
defined as the amount of substance in which 37 billion atoms per second undergo
radioactive disintegration. In the international system of units, the becquerel is the
preferred unit of radioactivity. One curie equals 3.7×10^{10} becquerels.

explosives are used to disperse radioactive material. Previous incidents involving radiological sources provide a measure of understanding for what could happen in the case of a dirty bomb attack. For example, in 1987, an accident involving an abandoned teletherapy machine, which is used to treat cancer by focusing a beam of radiation from a highly active radiological source at affected tissue, killed four people and injured more in central Brazil. The radiological source in the teletherapy device contained about 1,400 curies of cesium-137. The accident and its aftermath caused about $36 million in damages to the region, according to an official from Brazil's Nuclear Energy Commission. The accident significantly contaminated 85 houses and created environmental and medical problems. The decontamination process required the demolition of homes and other buildings and generated 3,500 cubic meters of radioactive waste. Furthermore, over 8,000 persons requested monitoring for contamination in order to obtain certificates stating they were not contaminated.

Concerns about thefts of radiological sources and the possible consequences of a dirty bomb attack persist. Their potential vulnerability to theft was highlighted in December 2013 when a truck in Mexico carrying a cobalt-60 source formerly used in medical treatment was stolen. Although the source was recovered 2 days later, officials from the National Nuclear Security Administration (NNSA), a separately organized semiautonomous agency within the Department of Energy (DOE), said that it was opened by the thieves, and they were uncertain whether the intended target of the theft was the truck or the source.

Furthermore, the Mexico case is not unique. According to the International Atomic Energy Agency (IAEA), there have been 615 confirmed incidents involving theft or loss of nuclear and radioactive materials around the world since 1993.[3] IAEA's Code of Conduct on the Safety and Security of Radioactive Sources serves as a guide to define high-risk radiological sources that warrant enhanced security and protection beyond what was applied before September 11, 2001. This includes Category 1 and Category 2 quantities of 16 radionuclides listed

---

[3]IAEA is an independent organization based in Vienna, Austria, that is affiliated with the United Nations and has the dual mission of promoting the peaceful uses of nuclear energy and verifying that nuclear materials intended for peaceful purposes are not diverted to military purposes.

in the Code of Conduct that pose the highest risk and thus warrant enhanced security and protection.[4]

The threat of an individual stealing a radiological source includes both an outsider and potential insider threat. According to the Federal Bureau of Investigation's (FBI) website, a company can often detect an outsider (nonemployee) and mitigate the threat of them stealing company property. However, the individual who is harder to detect is the insider— the employee with legitimate access.

The Nuclear Regulatory Commission (NRC) is responsible for licensing the commercial use of and regulating the security of radiological sources in the United States, including at industrial facilities. As part of its security role, NRC also issues legally binding requirements in the form of orders and regulations governing, among other things, the security of radiological sources. These controls address the need to secure these materials from outsider and insider threats. NRC may take enforcement actions against licensees who are found to have violated its regulations.[5] The actions may include notices of violation, monetary fines, or modifying, suspending, or revoking a license. In addition, 37 states are responsible for implementing licensing programs for industrial radiological sources, including security inspections—these states are referred to as "Agreement States."[6]

NNSA develops and implements policy and programs to prevent the proliferation of nuclear and radiological materials around the world. In 2008, NNSA established the Global Threat Reduction Initiative (GTRI)

---

[4]Within its categorization system, IAEA considers sources in Category 1 to be the most dangerous because they can pose a very high risk to human health if not managed safely and securely. Although the curie amount is less for Category 2 sources, they are also considered dangerous by IAEA.

[5]A licensee is a company, organization, institution, or other entity to which NRC or state agencies have granted a general license or specific license to construct or operate a nuclear facility, or to receive, possess, use, transfer, or dispose of source material, by-product material, or special nuclear material.

[6]42 U.S.C. § 2021(b) (2013). These states have entered into an agreement with NRC, whereby NRC has relinquished authority, and they have assumed regulatory authority over certain byproduct, source, and small quantities of special nuclear materials. Agreement States typically oversee radiological security through their state health or environment departments, and they inspect licensees to ensure compliance with state regulations that are generally compatible with NRC regulations.

domestic program, which among other things, provides security upgrades, such as motion sensors and alarms, to U.S. facilities with high-risk radiological sources beyond what NRC requires.[7] NNSA's program provides security upgrades only when requested by licensees and, as such, is a voluntary program. When requested, and subject to funding, NNSA assesses existing security conditions, recommends security enhancements, and funds the procurement and installation of jointly agreed-upon security measures that are consistent with best practices NNSA has identified. NNSA officials said that they would typically recommend that licensees (1) implement access controls, cameras, and critical remote monitoring systems; (2) relocate radiological sources to more secure locations at facilities; (3) install reinforced glass on interior windows that are in proximity to the source; and (4) cover or reinforce exterior openings such as skylights. Licensees are not required to implement NNSA's recommendations.

In addition to NRC and NNSA, the Department of Homeland Security (DHS) also plays a role in nuclear and radiological security. DHS is the primary federal agency for implementing domestic nuclear detection efforts for a managed and coordinated response to radiological and nuclear threats.

This report responds to your request that we review the security of radiological sources at U.S. industrial facilities. For this report, we evaluated (1) the challenges in reducing the security risks posed by high-risk industrial radiological sources and (2) the steps federal agencies are taking to ensure that high-risk industrial radiological sources are secured.

To conduct this work, we reviewed laws, regulations, and guidance related to the security of industrial radiological sources. We interviewed agency officials at NRC, NNSA, DHS, the Department of Transportation (DOT), and the United States Department of Agriculture (USDA). We also interviewed state government officials in three states, and safety and

---

[7]According to NNSA documents, the GTRI program partners with more than 100 countries to reduce and protect vulnerable nuclear and radiological material located at civilian sites worldwide. The program works to prevent terrorists from acquiring materials that could be used in a weapon of mass destruction, a crude nuclear bomb, a radiological dirty bomb, or other acts of terrorism. GTRI achieves its mission through three goals: convert research reactors and isotope production facilities from highly enriched uranium to low enriched uranium, remove and dispose of excess nuclear and radiological materials, and protect high-risk nuclear and radioactive materials from theft.

security personnel at 33 industrial facilities in six states, to obtain their views on how radiological sources are secured and what challenges they face in securing them. To identify thefts and incidents involving radiological sources we reviewed relevant documentation and spoke to federal and state officials. To determine the risks faced by industrial licensees of radiological sources, we visited 33 of about 1,400 industrial facilities in California, Colorado, Hawaii, Pennsylvania, Texas, and Wyoming. These facilities included 15 industrial radiography companies, 6 commercial or sterilization companies, 5 academic research facilities, 3 well logging companies, 2 manufacturing and distribution companies, and 2 USDA facilities. We selected these states and industrial facilities based on whether they were NRC states or Agreement States, the amount of curies contained in the devices using radiological sources, and the types of radiological devices. The facility information is not generalizable to all industrial facilities but provides illustrative examples. At the facilities, we observed the security measures in place and spoke to officials in charge of implementing NRC and Agreement State security controls and overseeing the security measures.

To evaluate the steps federal agencies are taking to ensure the radiological sources are secured at industrial facilities, we obtained information from and interviewed agency officials at NRC, NNSA, DOT, DHS, and USDA who are involved in securing sources and undertaking studies evaluating technologies related to source security. We also obtained information from Agreement States and NRC regions by reviewing documentation and interviewing officials at four Agreement States and one NRC regional office with responsibility for overseeing high-risk radiological sources. We selected these states and the NRC region based on the amount of curies and number of devices in the state containing radiological sources, the types of devices used, and geographic dispersion. We also interviewed officials at DOE's Pacific Northwest National Laboratory (PNNL) about the status of GTRI efforts made to strengthen remote tracking of mobile devices containing radiological sources. We visited industrial facilities that received NNSA funded upgrades and security assessments in California, Hawaii, and Pennsylvania. To determine the costs of these security upgrades, we obtained cost data from NNSA and interviewed the agency officials who manage the GTRI program. We discussed the reliability of these data with knowledgeable NNSA officials and questioned them about the system's controls to verify the accuracy and completeness of the data. We also analyzed these data for missing information and obvious outliers. We found the data sufficiently reliable for our reporting purposes. Appendix I presents a more detailed description of our scope and methodology.

We conducted this performance audit from November 2012 to June 2014 in accordance with generally accepted government auditing standards. Those standards require that we plan and perform the audit to obtain sufficient, appropriate evidence to provide a reasonable basis for our findings and conclusions based on our audit objectives. We believe that the evidence obtained provides a reasonable basis for our findings and conclusions based on our audit objectives.

Background

Radiological sources are used throughout the world for medical and industrial purposes. Until the 1950s, only naturally occurring radioactive materials, such as radium-226, were available for use in radiological sources. Since then, sources containing radioactive material produced artificially in nuclear reactors and accelerators have become widely available, including cesium-137, cobalt-60, and iridium-192. Sealed sources vary in size from the size of a grain of rice to rods up to several inches in length. Figure 1 provides an image of an americium-241 sealed radiological source.

Figure 1: Sealed Radiological Source That Contains Americium-241

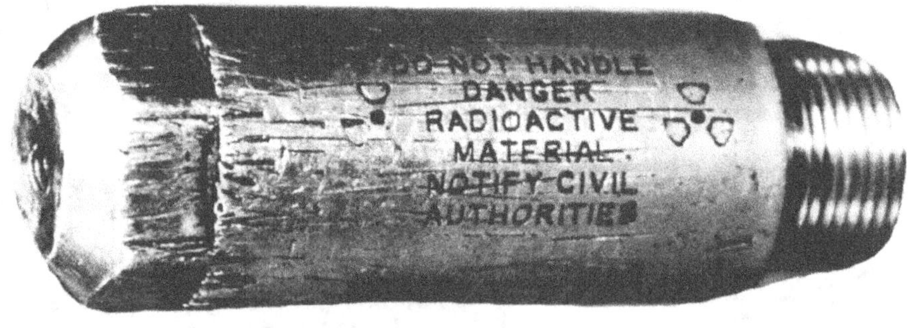

Source: DOE.

Note: This sealed source is not sized to scale.

According to IAEA, the level of protection provided by users of radioactive materials should be commensurate with the safety and security risks that the material presents if improperly used. For example, radioactive materials used for certain diagnostic imaging may not present a significant safety or security risk due to their low levels of activity. However, high-risk sealed radiological sources that contain cobalt-60, cesium-137, or iridium-192 could pose a greater threat to the public and the environment and a potentially more significant security risk, particularly if acquired by terrorists to produce a dirty bomb. Industrial radiological sources are used in, among other things: (1) industrial radiography devices for testing the integrity of welds, (2) well logging devices in oil and gas production, (3) research irradiators in the aerospace sector, and (4) panoramic and underwater irradiators used to sterilize industrial products.

NRC oversees licensees through three regional offices located in Pennsylvania, Illinois, and Texas. NRC has relinquished regulatory authority for licensing and regulating radiological sources to 37 Agreement States that have entered into an agreement with NRC. Figure 2 shows which states are overseen by NRC and which are Agreement States.

Figure 2: Map of Nuclear Regulatory Commission (NRC) Regions and 37 Agreement States

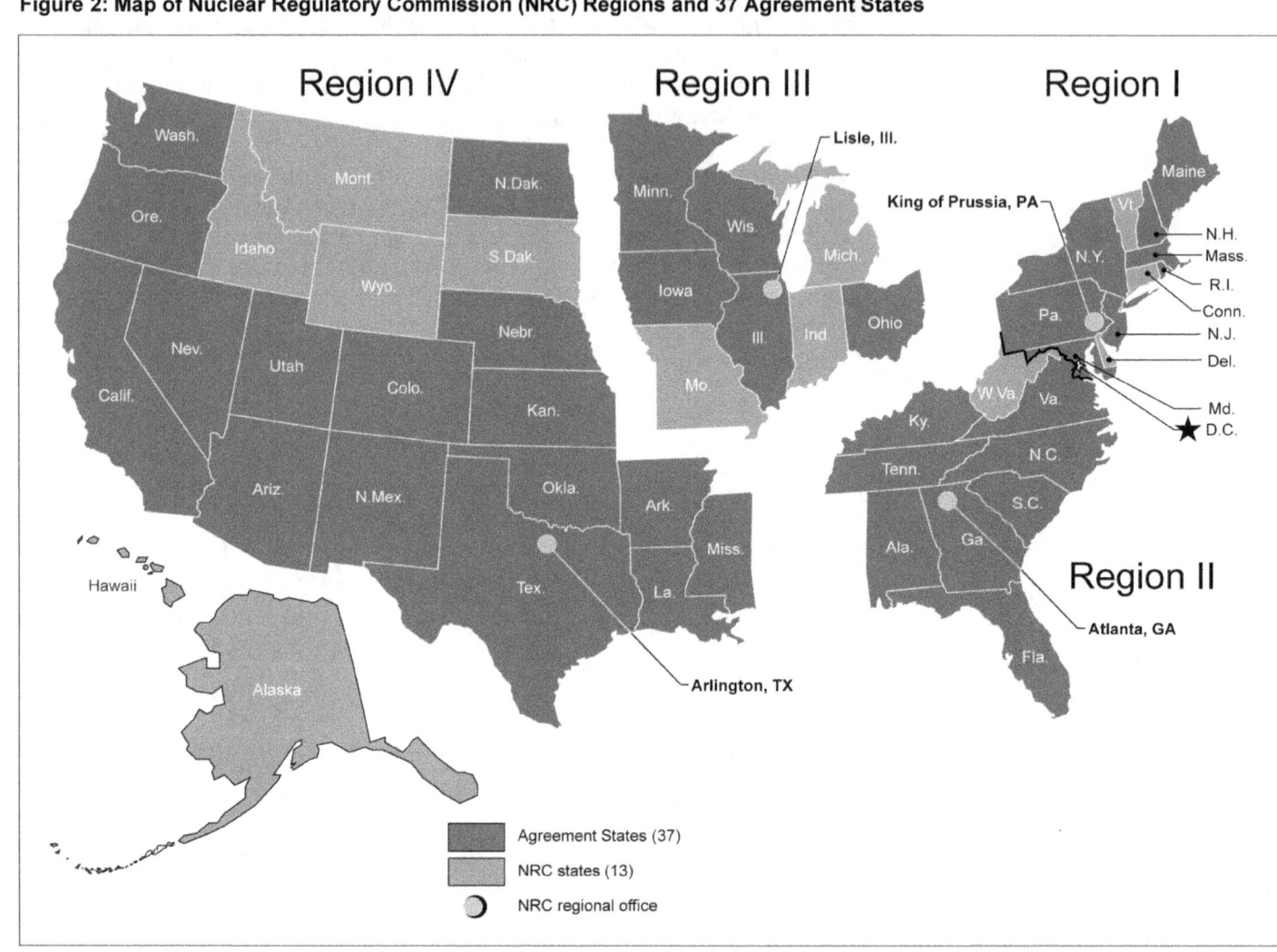

Sources: GAO; Map Resources (map).

Note: Although the figure depicts NRC's four regions, three of the four regions oversee licensees with radiological sources. Region I, located in Pennsylvania, oversees industrial facilities within Region II that have radiological sources. Regions III and IV oversee such facilities within their respective regions.

Prior to 2003, NRC did not have specific orders intended to address security, but its safety regulations included general provisions that licensees "secure from unauthorized removal or access" radiological sources in storage, and to "control and maintain constant surveillance" over materials not in storage.[8] Following the attacks of September 11, 2001, NRC determined that certain licensed material should be subject to specific security requirements.[9] The security of radioactive materials, or sources, is a stated top priority for the agency to prevent the use of such sources by terrorists. NRC has issued multiple orders and guidance documents that direct licensees possessing high-risk radiological sources to implement security measures. For the purposes of this report, we refer to these NRC security orders and implementation guidance as "NRC security controls" or "security controls." NRC's security controls apply to all types of high-risk industrial radiological sources, including mobile and stationary sources. These security controls include the following:

- A 2003 security order requiring increased security measures for licensees with panoramic and underwater irradiators.[10]

- A 2003 security order requiring increased security measures for licensees that manufacture and distribute radiological sources.[11]

- A 2005 security order directing all licensees possessing certain types of radiological materials, including those commonly used in industrial processes, to implement increased security measures, such as conducting employee background checks.[12] Implementation guidance was provided with the security order.[13]

---

[8]10 C.F.R. §§ 20.1801, 20.1802 (2014).

[9]NRC refers to the security controls as "increased" or "enhanced" controls, indicating an increased level of security after September 11, 2001, as compared with the safety requirements that provided some security.

[10]Order Imposing Compensatory Measures for All Panoramic and Underwater Irradiators Authorized to Possess Greater than 10,000 Curies of Byproduct Material in the Form of Sealed Sources. NRC Order EA-02-249.

[11]Order Imposing Additional Security Measures for all Licensees Authorized to Manufacture or Initially Transfer Items Containing Radioactive Material for Sale or Distribution and Possess High-Risk Radioactive Material of Concern. NRC Order EA-03-225.

[12]Order Imposing Increased Controls. NRC Order EA-05-090. NRC issues security orders to require licensees to implement interim security measures beyond what is currently required by NRC regulations and as conditions of licenses.

[13]Order Imposing Increased Controls. NRC Order EA-05-090, including Enclosures, Attachments, and Supplemental Questions and Answers.

- A 2007 security order requiring criminal background checks and fingerprinting for individuals needing unescorted access to radiological material for their jobs. Fingerprints are required to be sent to NRC, which forwards them to the FBI for criminal background checks.[14] Implementation guidance was also provided with this order.[15]

NRC officials told us that they have adopted a risk-based approach to security in which the level of security should be commensurate with the type and amount of sources that licensees are attempting to protect. According to NRC officials, the intent of the security controls is to develop a combination of people, procedures, and equipment that will delay and detect an intruder and initiate a response to the intrusion—not to provide absolute certainty that theft or unauthorized access will not be attempted, but to recognize and address such efforts should they occur. The security controls provide minimum requirements that must be met to ensure adequate security, and licensees may go beyond the minimum requirements.

NRC has recently taken action to codify its security orders and guidance into federal regulation. In March 2012, NRC approved the publication of final regulations to, among other things, establish requirements for security measures for medical and industrial radiological sources into NRC regulations, replacing the existing security orders. The final regulations, found in 10 C.F.R. Part 37 (commonly known as Part 37), were published in the *Federal Register* in March 2013, and they went into effect 60 days later.[16] NRC licensees were required to comply with the regulations by March 2014, while Agreement States are to promulgate compatible regulations by March 2016, with their licensees being required to comply at a subsequent date determined by each state. The current security orders remain in place until the new regulations are implemented. NRC has also developed and provided licensees with implementation

---

[14]Order Imposing Fingerprints. NRC Order EA-07-305.

[15]Order Imposing Fingerprints. NRC Order EA-07-305, including Supplemental Questions and Answers.

[16]NRC, Physical Protection of Byproduct Material; Final Rule, 78 Fed. Reg. 16,922 (Mar. 19, 2013) (amending and supplementing 10 C.F.R. Parts 20, 30, 32, et al.).

guidance for Part 37.[17] NRC officials said that a new round of security inspections would occur once the new regulations were in effect.

In September 2012,[18] we reported that, at the 26 selected hospitals and medical facilities we visited, NRC's requirements did not consistently ensure the security of high-risk radiological sources. One reason for this is that the requirements, which are contained in NRC security controls, are broadly written and do not prescribe specific measures that licensees must take to secure their equipment containing high-risk radiological sources. We recommended, among other things, that NRC strengthen its security controls by providing medical facilities with specific measures they must take to develop and sustain a more effective security program, including specific direction on the use of cameras and alarms. NRC disagreed that its security controls needed strengthening through more prescriptive security measures, stating that its approach provides adequate protection and gives licensees flexibility to tailor effective security measures across a wide variety of licensed facilities.

In contrast to NRC's flexible approach that allows licensees to determine which security measures to implement to meet the security controls, NNSA's voluntary program for radiological source security uses a prescriptive approach to upgrade the security of facilities—once a facility agrees to participate—to a level beyond NRC's minimum requirements. According to NNSA's physical security guidelines, which were established in 2010, the curie amounts for devices using high-risk radioactive material such as iridium-192, americium-241, and cesium-137 determine the level of protection required. For example, NNSA recommends that facilities using devices containing at least 10 curies of these materials upgrade, at a minimum, the security of doors, locks, windows, walls, and ventilation ducts. By comparison, NRC does not require security controls for some devices containing only 10 curies of iridium-192, americium-241, and cesium-137.[19] In addition, NNSA's guidelines for 10 curies and above

---

[17] *Implementation Guidance for 10 CFR Part 37, "Physical Protection of Category 1 and Category 2 Quantities of Radioactive Material"*, NUREG-2155.

[18] GAO, *Nuclear Nonproliferation: Additional Actions Needed to Improve Security of Radiological Sources at U.S. Medical Facilities*, GAO-12-925 (Washington, D.C.: Sept. 10, 2012).

[19] The NRC adopted the Category 1 and 2 threshold quantities from the IAEA Code of Conduct.

also call for video cameras, bullet resistant glass, hardened doors, cages, and security grating, and if possible, armed on-site response. For high-risk material totaling at least 1,000 curies, or when multiple smaller sources are located in the same storage facility with a combined curie level of 1,000 curies or more, NNSA recommends biometric access control devices, critical alarm remote monitoring systems, and enhanced barriers to delay an adversary's pathway to the radiological sources.

Challenges Exist in Reducing Security Risks for Different Types of Industrial Radiological Sources

Challenges exist in reducing the security risks faced by licensees using high-risk industrial radiological sources, even when they follow NRC's security controls. Specifically, licensees face challenges, in (1) securing mobile and stationary sources and (2) protecting against an insider threat.

Challenges in Reducing Risks for Mobile and Stationary Industrial Radiological Sources

We identified two main types of industrial radiological sources during the course of our review: mobile sources used for testing pipeline welds in the oil and gas sector, and stationary sources used for, among other things, aerospace research, oil and gas production, and food safety. Some of the stationary sources pose unique security challenges due to either how they are stored or their large curie levels. According to NNSA data, there are approximately 1,400 industrial facilities in the United States that house either mobile or stationary high-risk radiological sources, containing a combined total of approximately 126 million curies of radioactive material.[20]

Mobile Industrial Sources

The portability of some industrial radiological sources makes them susceptible to theft or loss. According to NRC, as of December 2013, there are approximately 498 radiography licensees with 4,162 radiological sources in the United States. These sources have a cumulative total of about 214,000 curies of primarily iridium-192 and cobalt-60. In 2007, we

---

[20]Regarding the number of industrial radiological sources in the United States, NRC bases its totals for sources and curie amounts on the number of licensees it has approved as of September 2013. They calculate that there are 793 total industrial licensees in the United States, containing approximately 129 million curies. NNSA bases its totals for sources and curie amounts on individual industrial facilities, i.e. buildings where the sources are located.

reported that IAEA officials said that transportation of high-risk radiological sources is the most vulnerable part of the nuclear and radiological supply chain.[21] Furthermore, according to IAEA documents, the size of some of these mobile sources could make it easier for unauthorized removal by an individual as the source is small enough to be placed into the pocket of a garment. The most common mobile source, iridium-192, is contained inside a small device called a radiography camera.[22] NRC officials said that the device is about the size of a gallon paint can and is transported in specially designed trucks to remote locations where it can remain in the field for days or even months. Figure 3 shows an example of a radiography camera.

---

[21]GAO, *Nuclear Nonproliferation: DOE's International Radiological Threat Reduction Program Needs to Focus Future Efforts on Securing the Highest Priority Radiological Sources*, GAO-07-282 (Washington, D.C.: Jan. 31, 2007).

[22]Radiographers use radiography devices, or cameras, to produce images used in the examination of structures such as pipelines. The cameras contain radioactive sealed sources. When the source is exposed, radiation penetrates the material and produces a shadow image on film or some other detection medium. Radiography cameras use sources that, if unshielded, are dangerous.

Figure 3: Industrial Radiography Camera

Source: GAO.

NRC's security controls call for two independent physical measures—such as two separate chains or steel cables locked and separately attached to the vehicle—when securing a mobile device containing a high-risk source to a truck.[23] The controls also call for licensees to maintain constant control and/or surveillance during transit, as well as disabling the truck containing such devices when not under direct control and constant surveillance by the licensee.[24] While the controls call for

---

[23]EA-05-090. For example, licensees may store their radiological sources in a box secured using two separate chains or steel cables that are locked and attached independently to the vehicle; the box also can be locked in a trunk or similar enclosure and secured further with a single locked chain or steel cable.

[24]NRC officials noted that NRC safety regulations for sealed sources in industrial radiography require the device and/or its container to be kept locked when not under the direct surveillance of a radiographer or assistant, and that when radiography is performed other than at a permanent radiographic installation, the radiographer must be accompanied by at least one other qualified individual. See 10 C.F.R. §§ 34.21(a), 34.41(a) (2014).

certain security measures, they do not include specific requirements for trucks to have alarm systems or specify the strength or robustness of the locks that must be used to secure the source inside the trucks. The controls also do not include requirements for a Global Positioning System (GPS) on the trucks.[25]

According to NRC officials, the agency's controls provide licensees with flexibility to meet the security requirements. For example, all of the 15 industrial radiography companies we visited implement different measures to secure their sources,[26] even though they use trucks with similar designs. Specifically, the trucks are distinguishable by a fiberglass enclosure sitting on the truck bed, which is known as a darkroom. At least one radiographer met NRC's controls with, among other things, a simple padlock on the door to the darkroom as the first security control, and an army surplus container chained to a cradle on the floor of the darkroom with a padlock as the second control. However, we also observed that other radiographers used high-security locks to control access to the darkroom, and reinforced metal containers that were bolted to the floor of the truck and secured using high-security locks. Of the 15 radiography companies we visited, 13 also had security alarms installed on their vehicles. However, we were told by 3 radiographers that the chemicals used inside the darkrooms to develop photographs of potential cracks in pipes can corrode the alarm systems, causing them to fail and requiring frequent service. Figures 4 and 5 show different methods radiographers we visited used to secure both the door to the darkroom and the radiological source while on the truck.

[25]GPS is a space-based satellite system that provides positioning, navigation, and timing data to users worldwide. As noted above, in 2013, NRC codified its security orders into regulation, with some revisions. The regulations, which licensees were not required to meet at the time of our visits, include a requirement that licensees use a telemetric position monitoring system or an alternative tracking system (such as, but not limited to, GPS) when transporting Category 1 quantities of radioactive material. 78 Fed. Reg. at 16924, 16937, 17018 (2013) (establishing 10 CFR § 37.79(a)(1)(iii). However, it should be noted that iridium-192 sources contained in radiography cameras are Category 2 and would not be covered under the tracking requirements contained in the new regulations.

[26]All of the 15 facilities we visited had implemented NRC's security controls according to the licensees and accompanying NRC or Agreement State inspector.

Figure 4: Standard Padlock for Darkroom Door and High-Security Lock for Door

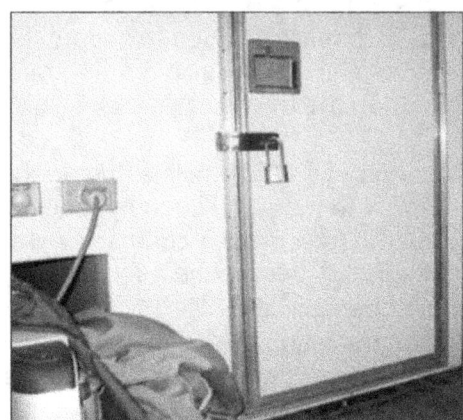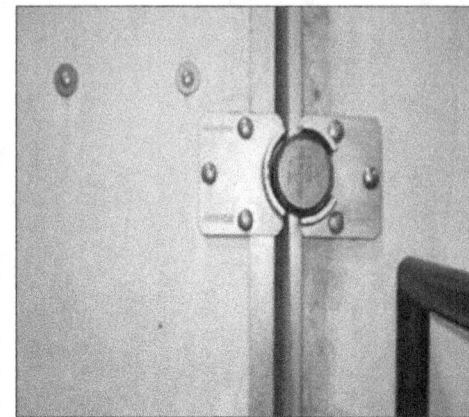

Source: GAO.

Figure 5: Radiography Camera Box Padlocked within Its Cradle and High-Security Box Bolted to the Floor of the Truck

Source: GAO.

The risks associated with mobile sources are underscored by a series of incidents involving both theft and unauthorized individuals attempting to gain access to the sources. We identified four cases in which radiological sources were stolen while on trucks since NRC's increased controls security order was issued in December 2005.[27] We also identified two cases of individuals impersonating state radiological safety and security inspectors at remote worksites where the mobile sources were being used.

Specifically regarding the theft of sources, according to NRC and Agreement State event reports we reviewed and interviews with NRC and Agreement State officials, we found that:

- In August 2012, a radiography camera containing 81 curies of iridium-192 was stolen from a truck parked outside of a company's facility in one state. An individual broke into five trucks, taking various items, including one radiography camera that had been left in one of the trucks rather than being returned to the storage facility. A surveillance camera identified the truck used by the individual, and police recovered the radiography camera from the individual's residence. Agreement State officials initially proposed fining the licensee $10,000, but the licensee and the state office ultimately settled on a fine of $1,000 to address the administrative penalty.

- In July 2011, a radiography camera containing 33.7 curies of iridium-192 was stolen from a truck parked in a hotel parking lot in the same state. Although the door to the truck's darkroom was locked and the device secured using cables and padlocks, the truck's alarm system was not activated. During the early morning hours, multiple individuals broke into the truck while it was parked at a motel and ripped the cables securing the container holding the radiography camera out of the wall of the darkroom enclosure. The radiological source was never recovered. The state initially proposed a $5,000 fine for the administrative penalty, but the penalty was reduced to $500 due to the efforts and expenses made by the company to recover the device.

- In September 2006, a radiography camera with approximately 100 curies of iridium-192 was stolen along with a radiography truck, which was parked at a gas station in the same state. The truck was stolen when the radiographer went into the gas station to talk with his supervisor and left the keys to the truck and the darkroom in the cab

---

[27]The trucks were generally equipped with security devices, such as locks, intended to meet NRC's security controls, and some had additional theft protection measures such as alarms.

of the truck. The truck was recovered 2 days later by the police at a nearby business park along with the radiological source. The state decided not to assess a fine against the company for the administrative penalty, noting that the device was recovered.

- In August 2006, a radiography camera with approximately 75 curies of iridium-192 was stolen along with a radiography truck from a hotel parking lot in another state. Although the truck was equipped with an alarm, the alarm was not activated. In addition, the radiographer left the vehicle's keys in the truck's door. The truck was abandoned and found the next day along with the radiological source by the police in a nearby strip mall parking lot. According to an Agreement State official, they do not have statutory authority to impose monetary fines for security violations, so no fine was assessed.[28]

Concerning individuals impersonating safety and security inspectors at remote worksites, according to incident reports we reviewed and state officials we spoke to, we found that:

- In September 2010, a radiography crew was approached at a temporary worksite by an individual who identified himself as an inspector. The individual became confrontational with the crew and approached the worksite. When the radiographers prevented him from entering the worksite, he accused them of violating proper procedures in their operation. The radiographers asked the individual to provide identification, but he refused and later left the worksite. The individual, who was a licensed radiographer, was identified as having multiple convictions on his record, including assault, forgery, and terroristic threats. The individual no longer practices radiography in the state.

- In March 2010, radiographers working at a temporary worksite were approached by an individual wearing a jacket with the state logo who identified himself as a safety and security inspector. The individual opened and closed the radiographer's truck doors, went into the darkroom, and then observed the radiographers as they performed operations. He asked the radiographers questions regarding the amount of curies in the radiography camera. After the radiographers

---

[28]An NRC official told us that several Agreement States do not legislatively empower their enforcement units to levy civil fines or penalties for violations.

contacted their superior, the individual left with two accomplices and was never apprehended.

Two radiography licensees, as well as an Agreement State and several NRC inspectors, told us that the existing security controls were adequate and that the industrial sources they use or monitor were adequately protected. For example, one licensee told us that—given the small size of his company, the company's limited financial resources, and the marginal risks associated with the radiological sources—additional security requirements were not necessary. In contrast, another Agreement State inspector told us that the security controls should be more prescriptive, as more specific controls would make selecting security measures clearer for licensees and evaluating the adequacy of such measures clearer for inspectors. He said that nonprescriptive controls require additional evaluation to determine if something is acceptable or not. In addition, a senior security official at a large radiography company told us that, prior to the July 2011 theft of the source that was never recovered, he believed that NRC's security controls were adequate. However, after the source was stolen, he concluded that NRC's controls needed to be more prescriptive. He told us that the controls are too general, which makes them largely ineffective. This official also said that the current playing field is not level and that some smaller radiography companies are doing a disservice to the radiography industry by installing security measures that meet NRC's security controls but are generally very weak. He cited several examples of security measures he has seen that he believes are substandard, including cheap locks, ineffective alarms, and darkroom doors that can be easily breached. This official recommended that industrial radiographers install common sense security measures, such as high-security locks, which cost approximately $50 each, reinforced doors, and GPS.

In addition, in 2007, the governor of Washington State requested that GPS should be required for licensees with highly radioactive mobile sources. Specifically, in 2006, the theft of a radiography camera in her state prompted the governor to petition NRC to consider requiring GPS for vehicles carrying high-risk sources, such as radiography cameras, or allow states the flexibility to implement more stringent security measures than those required by NRC. In the petition, the governor pointed to a separate incident where a smaller radioactive source in a portable gauge was stolen, but it was quickly recovered due to a GPS tracking feature on the phone of the operator. In response to the petition, NRC informed Washington State that the issues raised in the petition would be considered in the ongoing Part 37 rulemaking. However, in March 2013,

NRC denied the petitioner's request and did not require GPS tracking in the final Part 37 rule. NRC also stated in the *Federal Register* that, with respect to mobile radiological sources, existing security controls provide adequate protection for mobile devices and that GPS was "neither justified nor necessary."[29] An official from the Washington State's Department of Health stated in its response to NRC that his agency was very disappointed that the Part 37 rule did not follow through on the recommendation made by the governor and asserted that GPS tracking is inexpensive and an easy way to help with the rapid recovery of a stolen industrial radiological source should preventative measures fail.

Notwithstanding NRC's decision, some licensees that we met with during the course of our audit have installed GPS on their trucks. Of the 15 industrial radiography companies we visited, 8 had installed GPS on their fleet of trucks. Of these 8 companies, 4 also provided their radiographers with vibrating key fobs to alert them when the vehicle alarm goes off. In the view of the radiographers from these 8 companies, GPS is an effective security control. A senior security official at a large radiography company told us that, after learning about a theft in 2011, his company installed GPS in all 120 of its trucks at a cost of approximately $50 to $100 per installation and from $29 to $39 per truck for monthly service.

Stationary Industrial Sources

Securing stationary high-risk radiological sources also poses challenges for licensees. Facilities housing these sources include aerospace manufacturing and research plants, storage warehouses, and panoramic irradiators used to sterilize industrial products. Similar to the mobile sources, NRC's security controls for stationary sources provide a general framework that is implemented by the licensee. However, as we reported in September 2012,[30] the security controls are broadly written and do not provide specific direction on the use of cameras, alarms, and other relevant physical security measures.

The challenge that licensees face as a result of the broadly written security controls is that they may select from a menu of security measures, which allows them to meet NRC's controls but not necessarily address all potential security vulnerabilities. According to the licensees

---

[29]NRC, Physical Protection of Byproduct Material; Final Rule, 78 Fed. Reg. 16,922 (Mar. 19, 2013) (amending and supplementing 10 C.F.R. Parts 20, 30, 32, et seq.).

[30]GAO-12-925.

and inspectors that accompanied us, all of the industrial facilities with Category 1 and Category 2 high-risk radiological sources we visited had measures in place to meet NRC's security controls, such as locks and motion detectors, and the sources themselves were located within the interior of the building. While these facilities met NRC's security controls, we noted that some facilities appeared to continue to have certain vulnerabilities. For example, many of the facilities we visited did not have security measures of the type often recommended by NNSA as part of their voluntary security upgrades.[31] Examples of facilities we visited that met NRC's security controls but still had potential security vulnerabilities include the following:

- At one facility, we observed that a warehouse storing 25 iridium-192 radiography cameras had an exterior rolltop door that was open and unattended (see fig. 6). Once inside the warehouse, we also observed that the wall acting as one of the barriers to the sources did not go from the floor to the ceiling. When we asked the NRC security inspector who accompanied us about the barrier, the inspector told us that the licensee was in compliance with NRC's security controls because the sources were secured through other measures—such as locks and a motion detector. The inspector told us that while the security measures in place were not optimal, there were no apparent security violations.

- At another facility, we observed a cesium-137 irradiator with approximately 800 curies that was on wheels and in close proximity to a loading dock rollup door that was secured with a simple padlock (see fig. 7). The irradiator was stored in a vault that had a reinforced sliding door and a motion detector that was activated after normal working hours. The licensee told us that the wheels on the irradiator were needed to move the device to different parts of the facility when conducting research. During our visit, we observed that the sliding door to the vault—which is one of the security measures used by the licensee—was left open for ease of access. In our September 2012 report, we identified a similar situation at a medical facility and concluded that although the facility met NRC's security controls, it

---

[31]This is similar to the findings we reported in 2012 for medical facilities. All of the 26 medical facilities we visited at that time had implemented NRC's security controls and undergone inspections by either NRC or Agreement State inspectors. Although all of the facilities met NRC's security controls, more than half of these facilities had also received NNSA security upgrades or were in the process of receiving them for other vulnerabilities.

could be vulnerable because of the limited security we observed and the mobility of the irradiator.[32]

Figure 6: Open Rolltop Door and Barrier Not Extending to Ceiling

Source: GAO.

[32]GAO-12-925.

Figure 7: Irradiator on Wheels and Loading Dock

Source: GAO.

We also observed unsecured exterior skylights at a number of warehouses that contained radiological sources ranging from iridium-192 radiography cameras to higher curie levels of cobalt-60 and cesium-137 used for industrial research and manufacturing. Of the 33 industrial facilities we visited, 9 had unsecured skylights. When we questioned an NRC safety and security inspector who accompanied us on the visit about the unsecured skylights, he noted that the licensees met NRC's security controls because the sources were secured in a locked container, and he said that these skylights did not pose a security vulnerability. Figure 8 shows examples of unsecured skylights.

Figure 8: Unsecured Skylights at Industrial Facilities

Source: GAO.

We also identified two types of stationary sources that pose unique security challenges due to (1) how americium-241 sources are currently being stored at some well logging facilities and (2) the large curie levels of cobalt-60 sources found in panoramic irradiators.

Well Logging Storage Facilities

Well logging is a process used to determine whether a well has the potential to produce oil. Some well logging storage facilities with large amounts of americium-241, including two facilities that we visited, are potentially more vulnerable to theft as they have not implemented NRC's security controls.[33] Under NRC's security controls, increased security measures are triggered by the type and amounts of curies of radiological sources. For example, licensees with americium-241 are required to implement NRC's security controls when the radiological sources in their possession total 16 curies or more. Under the security controls, multiple sources of the same type are added together for regulatory purposes only

---

[33]According to NNSA, there are approximately 1,736 well logging sources in the United States, with almost 13,000 curies of primarily americium-241 and cesium-137—2 of the 16 radiological sources posing the highest risk and thus warranting enhanced security.

if they are "collocated."[34] NRC considers these sources to be collocated if someone could gain access to them by breaching a single physical barrier. However, some well logging licensees do not come under NRC's security controls because they separate their americium-241 into quantities that are not considered collocated. For example, these licensees may store quantities of this source in multiple separately locked containers, which function as barriers, so they do not meet the definition of being collocated. Figure 9 shows an example how licensees could store americium-241 in separate containers that would not be considered collocated, and therefore, not under NRC's controls. As a result, a segment of facilities with large quantities of radiological sources falls outside of NRC's increased security controls, including security inspections for the increased controls.[35] As mentioned earlier, NRC has identified the security of radioactive sources as a top agency priority to prevent the use of such sources by terrorists. Thus, NRC's definition of collocation may have the unintended consequence of placing a segment of these sources at greater risk of theft or loss.

---

[34]The 2013 regulations continue this distinction. See, e.g., 78 Fed. Reg. at 17,007 (adding § 37.5 defining aggregated), 17014 (adding §37.41(a)(1) incorporating aggregated quantities into the applicability of physical protection requirements). NRC has explained, "[a] licensee may choose to store radioactive materials, in any form, in separate locations to avoid being subject to the proposed security requirements. Such action would not conflict with the intent of the proposed rule, which is to limit access to an aggregated category 2 [i.e., high-risk] quantity of radioactive material." 78 Fed. Reg. at 16,997.

[35]All licensed material is subject to NRC's and Agreement State requirements for storage and control of licensed materials. (See 10 C.F.R. 20.1801 and 20.1802.) The level of security and type of security inspection varies based on the type of material the licensee possesses and how the licensee stores the material.

Figure 9: Well Logging Storage Facility with Multiple Containers for Storing Radiological Sources

Source: National Nuclear Security Administration.

Note: As figure 9 shows, the multiple in-ground containers store the radioactive materials, which in some cases can contain americium-241 below the levels that require increased security controls.

We visited two well logging storage facilities and observed quantities of americium-241 totaling greater than 16 curies that were stored in such a way as not to be considered collocated—and therefore not subject to NRC's security controls or their enforcement by either NRC or Agreement State inspectors. NRC and Agreement State officials told us that well logging licensees are not purposely avoiding NRC's security controls. Furthermore, in their view, the security controls are adequate. Notwithstanding those views, an NNSA official stated that the security measures employed by some well loggers could put the sources at risk. NNSA is planning to evaluate the potential risks posed by these sources and determine how best to secure them.

Panoramic Irradiator Facilities

Many panoramic irradiators used to sterilize industrial products have high curie levels of cobalt-60 and are located near urban areas. According to NNSA officials, there are currently 55 panoramic irradiators in the United States. Panoramic irradiators generally utilize "source racks" that hold hundreds of thousands to millions of curies of cobalt-60. The source rack is composed of individual source "pencils" containing several thousand curies of cobalt-60 each. NNSA officials told us that when in use (raised out of a pool of water used to shield the source) the radiation produced by the entire source rack is strong enough to incapacitate a human in a matter of minutes. When not in use (lowered into the pool of water), individual pencils could potentially be targeted for theft.

In one state, we visited two facilities operated by the two largest panoramic irradiator companies in the United States. One of the facilities had two cobalt-60 panoramic irradiators, one with 5 million curies and one with 2.2 million curies. The other facility had one panoramic irradiator with 2 million curies of cobalt-60. Both of these facilities were located near large urban areas. NRC has security controls in place for industrial facilities with large-scale irradiators to specify minimum security controls.[36] To meet these controls, the companies we visited have installed, among other things, video cameras, motion detectors, and key pad locks. Nevertheless, NNSA officials, who have visited similar facilities at both companies, told us that the large curie levels used in the irradiators and proximity to urban areas still creates potential security risks despite the security measures already implemented. As a result, NNSA has recommended a number of security upgrades for panoramic irradiators, including: (1) installing alarmed pool covers; (2) installing enhanced access controls including biometric devices and alarm systems focused on the irradiator; and (3) installing remote monitoring systems. Figure 10 shows a photograph of exterior doors at a panoramic irradiator facility we visited.

---

[36] Order Imposing Compensatory Measures for All Panoramic and Underwater Irradiators Authorized to Possess Greater than 370 TerraBecquerels (10,000 Curies) of Byproduct Material in the Form of Sealed Sources. EA-02-249.

Figure 10: Loading Dock with Roll up Doors

Source: GAO.

Licensees Face Challenges Protecting Against an Insider Threat

Licensees of mobile and stationary radiological sources face challenges in determining which of their employees are suitable for trustworthiness and reliability (T&R) certification, as required by NRC's security controls.[37] Such certification allows for unescorted access to high-risk radiological sources. Officials at almost half of the facilities we visited told us that they face challenges in making T&R determations. These challenges include limited security experience and training and incomplete information to determine an employee's suitability for unescorted access.

Before a licensee can grant an employee unescorted access to high-risk radiological sources, NRC security controls require the licensee, among other things, to: (1) conduct employment and education background

---

[37]As noted above, our report focuses on the security controls that were in place during our 2013 visits to licensees. With respect to T&R certification, the Part 37 regulations now in effect continue the same approach as the prior security controls. Where appropriate, we reference the Part 37 regulations and implementing guidance.

checks; (2) perform an identification and criminal history check that includes taking the employee's fingerprints and sending them to NRC, which forwards the fingerprints to the FBI; and (3) determine that the individual is trustworthy and reliable. These controls are intended to mitigate the risk of an insider threat—an employee or someone else with authorized access who might be trying to steal, tamper with, or sabotage radiological sources. NNSA officials told us that they consider an insider threat to be the primary threat to facilities with radiological sources. According to an NNSA Fact Sheet, almost all known cases of theft of nuclear and radiological material involved an insider. The document states that skills, knowledge, access, and authority held by some insiders make the threat difficult to mitigate. As a result, great care must be taken in determining the T&R of employees who are granted unescorted access in facilities with high-risk radiological sources.

Under NRC's security controls, the criminal history check is performed by the FBI, submitted to NRC, and forwarded to the licensee. NRC's controls place the responsibility on the licensee to evaluate all the information and determine whether the employee is trustworthy and reliable. In its Part 37 regulations, NRC codified the process for criminal history check and review generally as established in the orders. In response to its proposal for these regulations, NRC received comments stating that it should provide specific criteria—such as disqualifying convictions—for use by licensees with respect to the T&R determination. However, NRC declined to provide specific criteria, stating that it is the licensee's responsibility to consider all information and make a determination. An NRC official told us that this was a policy choice by the Commission. The official said that NRC's role in the T&R determinations is limited, but NRC inspectors may review a licensee's records during a site inspection. However, the official told us that such a review is limited to whether the licensee obtained the required types of information, not the merits of the licensee's determination to grant unescorted access to an individual.

NRC has provided licensees with a number of indicators to consider when evaluating an individual's T&R. Some of these include the following:

- conduct that warrants referral for criminal investigation or results in arrest or conviction;

- uncontrolled anger, violation of safety or security procedures, or repeated absenteeism;

- attempted or threatened destruction of property or life; and

- the frequency and recency of the conduct.

NRC implementation guidance states that these indicators are not meant to be all inclusive or be disqualifying factors. Moreover, NRC's guidance states that it is a licensee's business decision as to what criteria it uses for the basis of the T&R determination.[38] NRC guidance—as well as its new regulations—does not specify how a licensee should evaluate an individual's T&R. For example, NRC's current and former implementation guidance do not include indicators that would disqualify an employee from receiving unescorted access. Instead, each case must be judged on its own merits, and final determination remains the responsibility of the licensee. NRC's implementation guidance also states that the requirements are not intended to stop determined adversaries intent on malevolent action from gaining access to the radioactive sources. Rather, this implementation guidance is designed to provide reasonable assurance that individuals with unescorted access to the radiological sources are trustworthy and reliable and that facilities have a reliable means to monitor events that are potentially malevolent and have a process for prompt police response.

Under NRC's security controls, it is left to the licensee to decide whether to grant unescorted access, even if an individual has been indicted or convicted for a violent crime or terrorism, and the licensee is not required to consult with NRC before granting T&R access. Officials at 7 of the 33 licensees we reviewed said that they have granted unescorted access to high-risk radiological sources to individuals with criminal histories. We found two cases where employees of industrial radiographers in two different states were granted unescorted access despite having serious criminal records.

- *Case 1: Individual with numerous criminal convictions.* In one case, a T&R official told us that she granted unescorted access to an individual in 2008 with an extensive criminal history, some of which was included on the FBI report the company received from NRC, and

---

[38]The current guidance similarly states, "it should be left to the licensee's judgment whether criminal arrests indicate poor judgment, unreliability, or untrustworthiness." Implementation Guidance for Part 37, "Physical Protection of Category 1 and Category 2 Quantities of Radioactive Material," NUREG-2155, pp.120-121. Prior to this guidance, which accompanied the new 2013 regulation, NRC had provided licensees with similar guidance in various documents.

some that was absent. This criminal history included two convictions for terroristic threat that occurred in 1996, which were not included in the background information provided to the T&R official by NRC. While NRC's security orders do not preclude granting unescorted access to radiological sources to persons with convictions for terroristic activity (or other serious crimes), the T&R official said that had she been aware of the individual's convictions for terroristic threat, she would not have granted him unescorted access. Based on available documents, we identified that the individual had been arrested and convicted multiple times between 1996 and 2008. These convictions included the following: terroristic threat (twice), assault, forgery, failure to appear in court, driving while intoxicated, and driving with a suspended license. According to that state's statute, a terroristic threat includes any offense involving violence to any person or property with intent to, among other things: place the public or a substantial group of the public in fear of serious bodily injury; place any person in fear of imminent serious bodily injury; or prevent or interrupt the occupation or use of a building, place of assembly, place of employment or occupation, aircraft, automobile, or other form of conveyance.[39] According to NRC officials, identification of a criminal history through the FBI or a discretionary local criminal history check does not automatically indicate unreliability or untrustworthiness of an individual. The licensee may authorize individuals with criminal records for unescorted access to radioactive materials notwithstanding the individual's criminal history.

In 2010, the individual was declared to be a substantial threat by the Agreement State's licensing agency after he impersonated a radiography inspector and was hostile toward radiographers in the field, as previously discussed. An investigation performed by the state health department concluded that the individual was a threat to public health and safety, and he subsequently surrendered his state radiography license. It was not clear from available information why the terroristic threats and other convictions did not appear on the FBI criminal background check or why the official deemed the individual trustworthy and reliable. We brought this case to NRC's attention after learning about it in February 2014. In response, NRC officials said

---

[39]NRC indicated that the terroristic threat convictions were based on a violent verbal threat that the individual made against two other individuals, not the United States. Making this type of "terroristic threat" is a misdemeanor offense.

that they contacted the Agreement State office to gather relevant information and independently evaluate whether the situation represented an isolated incident or if it was indicative of a programmatic issue. Based on their initial review, the officials said that they believed the event was an isolated incident. However, without an assessment of the T&R process, NRC will not be able to determine the extent to which this case may represent a larger problem or if corrective actions are needed.

- *Case 2: Individual caught stealing from company.* In another case, an industrial radiographer in charge of making T&R determinations told us that an individual with an extensive criminal record was granted unescorted access to radiological sources. The T&R official told us that he considered the individual a risk and objected to granting him unescorted access, but he was overruled by his supervisor. The employee who had been granted access was subsequently arrested for stealing from the company.

Without more complete information and specific guidance on how to evaluate an individual's T&R, licensees could continue to face challenges in making decisions about the suitability of personnel who are granted unescorted access to high-risk radiological sources, elevating the risk of an insider threat, which NNSA has identified as being responsible for almost all known cases of theft of nuclear and radiological material. As noted above, NRC's approach to providing reasonable assurance to an insider threat is to require licensees to collect and to consider various types of information, including an FBI criminal history, and to make a determination based on the licensee's judgment, without any NRC-identified disqualifying criteria. Therefore, nothing in the NRC controls or guidance precluded the licensees in these two examples from approving access. Moreover, according to an NRC official, NRC's role is limited to providing guidance and inspecting that the licensee has accumulated all appropriate information when making T&R determinations—not the merits of any particular decisions.

Federal Agencies Are Taking Steps to Improve Security of Radiological Sources but Are Not Always Effectively Collaborating

Federal agencies are taking steps to better secure industrial radiological sources. Specifically, NRC is developing a Best Practices Guide for licensees of high-risk radiological sources and planning to provide additional training to NRC inspectors. In addition, NNSA has two initiatives under way to improve industrial radiological source security. However, NRC, NNSA, and DHS—agencies that play a role in nuclear and radiological security—are not effectively collaborating to achieve the common mission of securing mobile industrial sources.

NRC Is Developing a Best Practices Guide and Planning Additional Security Training for Inspectors

NRC plans to develop a Best Practices Guide for licensees of high-risk radiological sources in response to a recommendation in our September 2012 report.[40] According to NRC officials, the guide is expected to be issued in spring 2014 and will include information for licensees on physical barriers; locks; monitoring systems, such as cameras and alarms; as well as examples of how to secure mobile sources and sources in transit. NRC officials told us that the guide will serve as a layperson's source of practical information about security and have minimal technical language. However, the Best Practices Guide remains in draft form, and it is not clear that it will provide specific direction on cameras, alarms, and other relevant physical security measures. For example, the officials said that the guide will not be a catalogue for specific makes and models of security devices such as cameras and locks.

During development of the Best Practices Guide, an NRC official told us that they are relying on a working group that includes, among others, representatives from NNSA, four inspectors from NRC's regional offices, one Agreement State inspector, and one Agreement State manager to provide insight into challenges licensees face in complying with NRC's security controls. However, the official also told us that they have not directly reached out to licensees during the development of the Best Practices Guide. NRC data show that there are almost 800 industrial licensees in the United States.

---

[40]GAO-12-925.

As we reported in 2013, active engagement with program stakeholders is a critical factor to success.[41] Furthermore, in 2012, we reported that programs are most likely to succeed when they involve stakeholders in establishing shared expectations for the outcome of the process.[42] According to professional practices, project managers should identify and prioritize stakeholders to include those who will be directly affected (positively and negatively) by the project.[43] Once the stakeholders are identified, continuous communication is needed to ensure that their needs are understood, issues are addressed as they come up, and they are engaged in the project decisions and activities. Although developing the guide is a step in the right direction, without including the views of licensees, NRC cannot be certain that the guide will be as useful as it could for those who will be directly affected by the process.

NRC also plans to provide additional security training for NRC and Agreement State inspectors to improve security awareness and reinforce a security culture. For example, NRC began revising the inspector training course in May 2013 and moved the training facility from Sandia National Laboratories to the NRC Technical Training Center in Chattanooga, TN. NRC officials told us that the course will provide information on physical protection systems and NRC security controls, including the identification of threats, an introduction to physical protection systems, and the identification of critical components of physical security, such as detection and access control. NRC officials also said that they have built a mock security laboratory at the Technical Training Center, which includes examples of security equipment such as security sensors, alarms, locks, and cameras. In addition, NRC plans to take inspectors on facility tours to introduce them to security practices at an irradiator site that has installed the voluntary NNSA security upgrades, a small mobile radiography company, and a local emergency response center.

---

[41]GAO, *Information Technology: Leveraging Best Practices to Help Ensure Successful Major Acquisitions*, GAO-14-183T (Washington, D.C.: Nov. 13, 2013).

[42]GAO, *DHS Strategic Workforce Planning: Oversight of Departmentwide Efforts Should Be Strengthened*, GAO-13-65 (Washington, D.C.: Dec. 3, 2012).

[43]"A Guide to the Project Management Body of Knowledge," Project Management Institute, 2013. "Eight Strategies for Research to Practice," fhi 360, September 2012.

NNSA Efforts to Address Security Risks Posed by Industrial Radiological Sources

NNSA has two initiatives under way to address security risks posed by industrial radiological sources: (1) testing and developing tracking technology for mobile sources, and (2) upgrading the physical security of industrial facilities.

Testing and developing technology for tracking mobile sources. In 2013, NNSA officials reported spending approximately $800,000 for a project to develop tracking systems for mobile devices containing radiological sources. Under cost-sharing arrangements, NNSA officials told us that they are collaborating with industry partners from both the industrial radiography and well logging industries who have agreed to provide support for development, design reviews, and field testing of prototype systems. According to the officials, this technology, if successful, would allow for (1) real-time tracking and monitoring of the source in storage, during transport, and during temporary storage within the transport vehicle, (2) immediate notification of a potential loss or theft situation to a central monitoring location, and (3) assistance in recovering a source that is lost or stolen. NNSA officials said that they plan to complete the development of the tracking systems and transfer the technology to one or more vendors for commercial manufacture and sale by summer 2015. Individual industrial radiography and well logging companies would be able to purchase the systems directly from the commercial manufacturer. To encourage use of the technology, NNSA is also evaluating if the government should subsidize all or a portion of the cost of the systems and, if so, for all potential users, or a particular group of users meeting certain criteria. NNSA officials told us that they expect the systems to cost in the range of $300 to $500 for each radiography device, and $500 to $750 for each well logging truck.

Security upgrades at facilities. As of June 2013, NNSA had completed security upgrades at 20 industrial facilities at a cost of $5.5 million. Included in the 20 industrial facilities with completed upgrades are 7 USDA sites with irradiators containing cobalt-60 and cesium-137 that are used for research and pest irradiation. Upgrade of these 7 facilities cost $3.8 million. NNSA has also completed security upgrades at one mobile radiography facility but, according to NNSA officials, the agency decided not to upgrade any additional facilities because higher priority facilities were scheduled for completion first. In addition, NNSA officials said that their current plans are to complete the development of the electronic mobile source tracking system prior to implementing security upgrades at additional radiography storage facilities. They told us that security at storage facilities for mobile sources would only address half the risk, as the sources also travel into the field.

NNSA's activities include working with federal, state, and local agencies, as well as private industry to install sustainable security enhancements for high-priority nuclear and radiological materials located at civilian sites in the United States. However, an NNSA official told us that, in light of their available funds for these efforts, many of these civilian sites with industrial radiological sources have not received security upgrades, and it is uncertain when or if such upgrades will be made. To date, NNSA has focused most of its attention and planning—and expended the majority of available funds for making such upgrades—on U.S. medical facilities. As of June 2013, NNSA had completed security upgrades at approximately one-quarter of all U.S. hospitals and medical facilities with high-risk radiological sources at a total cost of $135 million. NNSA officials said that the agency's focus on medical facilities is due primarily to the large number of facilities that, in their view, pose a more immediate risk because they are located in and around urban areas, contain large quantities of high-risk sources, and include buildings that are generally more accessible to the general public. However, these officials said that, as the number of medical facilities left to upgrade decreases, the program has begun to focus on industrial facilities and is finding that these facilities (particularly in the panoramic irradiation, industrial radiography, and well logging industries) may require unique security solutions and an updated budget estimate.

Federal Agencies Are Not Always Effectively Collaborating on Technology Development

Although DHS, NNSA, and NRC have an interagency mechanism for collaborating on, among other things, radiological security, they were not always doing so effectively. By not having effective ways to ensure consistent collaboration, the agencies may be missing opportunities to achieve the common mission of securing radiological sources. Our previous work has identified that when responsibilities cut across more than one federal agency—as they do for securing industrial radiological sources—it is important for agencies to work collaboratively.[44] Taking into account the nation's long-range fiscal challenges, we noted that the federal government must identify ways to deliver results more efficiently and in a way that is consistent with its multiple demands and limited resources. In addition, we have previously reported on the need for collaboration in securing radiological sources. For example, we reported

---

[44]GAO, *Practices That Can Help Enhance and Sustain Collaboration among Federal Agencies*, GAO-06-15 (Washington, D.C.; Oct. 21, 2005).

in 2007, that while DOE has improved coordination with the Department of State and NRC to secure radiological sources worldwide, DOE has not always integrated its efforts efficiently, and coordinated efforts among the agencies have been inconsistent.[45]

During this review, we found that the agencies involved in securing radiological sources—DHS, NNSA, and NRC—meet quarterly, along with the FBI, for "trilateral" meetings that include, among other things, discussions of radiological security. However, these meetings did not help DHS, NNSA, and NRC collaborate and draw on each agency's expertise during research, development, and testing of new technology for a mobile source tracking device. Specifically, we found that DHS contracted with Sandia National Laboratories in October 2011 to study commercially available technologies for tracking mobile radiological sources.[46] The cost of the study was $271,000. The study concluded that it is physically possible to tag some radiography and oil well logging devices. However, existing technology such as GPS—as opposed to developing a new technology—has limitations that would prevent reliable or effective tracking. DHS collaborated with NRC and several DOE national laboratories to develop the study but did not share the results with key NNSA officials who are directly involved in radiological source security. According to DHS officials, they made NNSA aware of the report through their quarterly meetings of senior officials, but NNSA officials with responsibility for securing radiological sources told us that they were not aware of the report until we brought it to their attention during the course of our review. NNSA officials told us that it would have been helpful to have the report earlier. As a result, the officials had to quickly evaluate the report's findings to ensure there were no "show stoppers" that would negatively impact their current activities in the same area of technology development.

---

[45]GAO-07-282.

[46]R.K. Patel and B.K. Smith, DNDO Feasibility Study of Electronically Tagging and Tracking Portable Radiation Radiography and Oil Well Logging Sources. SAND2010-6905, Sandia National Laboratories, Albuquerque, NM, 2010. DOE oversees the largest laboratory system of its kind in the world. The mission of DOE's 23 national laboratories has evolved over the last 55 years. Originally created to design and build atomic bombs under the Manhattan Project, these national laboratories have since expanded to conduct research in many disciplines—from high-energy physics to advanced computing at facilities throughout the nation. Nine of DOE's laboratories are large, multiprogram national laboratories that dominate DOE's science and technology activities.

NNSA is also developing a tracking system for devices containing mobile radiological sources, such as industrial radiography cameras. However, we found that NNSA has not been collaborating with DHS and NRC on the project. For example, NNSA did not reach out to DHS for input regarding tracking technologies, even though DHS had completed a related study in 2011 concerning tracking mobile radiological sources (see above). Regarding NRC, NNSA officials told us that they have no plans to coordinate with the NRC division in charge of regulating and licensing radiological sources—the division that has regulatory authority for radiological security. NNSA officials stated that they would reach out to the NRC technical division that approves and certifies changes in the design of the packaging and transportation of the device. However, the officials noted that coordination would only occur if NNSA determined that recertification of the device is required, which they believed was not likely.

As we have previously found, collaborating agencies should identify the human, information technology, physical, and financial resources needed to initiate or sustain their collaborative effort.[47] The current collaboration mechanism employed by DHS, NNSA, and NRC appears to not always be effective, and it may contribute to missed opportunities to leverage resources, including expertise, in developing new technology to address vulnerabilities associated with radiological sources while in transit.

Conclusions

Federal agencies are taking steps to better secure industrial radiological sources in the United States. Nevertheless, we found that licensees still face challenges in securing these sources. NRC is developing a Best Practices Guide to reduce the risks posed by the sources and thus help inform and educate licensees and other stakeholders about measures that could be taken to raise the level of security awareness and improve security. While this is a positive step, NRC has not directly reached out to licensees to obtain their views. Active engagement with key stakeholders is a leading practice on which we and others have reported. Without including the views of licensees, NRC cannot be certain that the guide will be as useful as it could for those who will be directly affected by the process.

---

[47]GAO-06-15.

NRC requires security controls for radiological sources commensurate with the type and amount of sources that licensees are attempting to protect. However, some well logging licensees do not come under NRC's increased security controls, because they separate their americium-241 into quantities that do not meet NRC's definition of collocation. Because these facilities fall outside of NRC's increased security controls, they do not receive security inspections for the increased controls. As a result, a segment of these sources are potentially at greater risk of theft or loss.

In addition, licensees are required to make T&R determinations regarding employee suitability to have unescorted access to high-risk radiological sources. Under NRC's security controls, even if an individual has been indicted or convicted for a violent crime, the licensee is not required to consult with NRC before granting unescorted access to high-risk sources. It is unclear whether two cases where employees were granted unescorted access, even though each had extensive criminal histories—including, in one of the cases, convictions for terroristic threats—represent isolated incidents or a systemic weakness in the T&R process. Without an assessment by NRC, the agency may not have "reasonable assurance" that the process in place to make access decisions is as robust as it needs to be to prevent the theft or diversion of high-risk radiological sources by a determined insider. NRC's security controls are also silent on what, if any, indicators would disqualify an employee from being granted unescorted access. Without more complete information and specific guidance on how to evaluate T&R, licensees could continue to face challenges in making decisions about the suitability of personnel who are granted unescorted access to high-risk radiological sources, potentially increasing the risk of an insider security threat, which NNSA has identified as being responsible for almost all known cases of theft of nuclear and radiological material.

As we have reported in the past, it is important for agencies to work collaboratively to achieve greater efficiency. An interagency mechanism exists to promote collaboration among the agencies responsible for securing radiological sources. However, DHS, NRC, and NNSA have missed the opportunity to leverage resources, including expertise, in developing a new technology to track radiological sources, which could aid in the timely recovery of a lost or stolen radiological source and support the agencies' common mission.

Recommendations for Executive Action

We are making four recommendations in this report.

To ensure that the security of radiological sources at industrial facilities is reasonably assured, we recommend that the Chairman of the Nuclear Regulatory Commission take the following three actions:

- Obtain the views of key stakeholders, such as licensees, during the development of the Best Practices Guide to ensure that the guide contains the most relevant and useful information on securing the highest risk radiological sources.

- Reconsider whether the definition of collocation should be revised for well logging facilities that routinely keep radiological sources in a single storage area but secured in separate storage containers.

- Conduct an assessment of the T&R process—by which licensees approve employees for unescorted access—to determine if it provides reasonable assurance against insider threats, including

  - determining why criminal history information concerning convictions for terroristic threats was not provided to a licensee during the T&R process to establish if this represents an isolated case or a systemic weakness in the T&R process; and

  - revising, to the extent permitted by law, the T&R process to provide specific guidance to licensees on how to review a employee's background. NRC should also consider whether certain criminal convictions or other indicators should disqualify an employee from T&R or trigger a greater role for NRC.

To better leverage resources, including expertise, to address vulnerabilities associated with radiological sources while in transit, we recommend that the Administrator of NNSA, the Chairman of NRC, and the Secretary of DHS review their existing collaboration mechanism for opportunities to enhance collaboration, especially in the development and implementation of new technologies.

Agency Comments and Our Evaluation

We provided a draft of this report to the Chairman of the NRC, the Administrator of NNSA, and the Secretary of Homeland Security for review and comment. NNSA and NRC provided written comments on the draft report, which are presented in appendices II and III, respectively. DHS did not provide comments. NRC generally agreed with our four recommendations, and NNSA agreed with the one recommendation directed to it to enhance collaboration with other federal agencies on the development and implementation of new technologies. In its written comments, NNSA also said that it is ready to support NRC efforts with technical expertise and other assistance as required in relation to the recommendations directed toward NRC. NRC and NNSA also provided technical comments that we incorporated as appropriate. In addition, the Organization of Agreement States, which represents the 37 Agreement States responsible for overseeing regulatory compliance for radiological sources, provided technical comments.

In its written comments, NRC stated that the security and control of radioactive sources is a top priority and that its regulations provide a framework that requires licensees to develop security programs with measures specifically tailored to their facilities. NRC also noted that its inspectors have already investigated and taken action on some of our concerns identified in the report regarding the use of industrial sources, and if additional measures are needed, it will consider appropriate enhancements. NRC agreed with our recommendations to (1) obtain the views of stakeholders during development of its Best Practices Guide and (2) enhance collaboration with other federal agencies on the development and implementation of new technologies. NRC also acknowledged the merits of the two other recommendations to reconsider the definition of collocation for well logging facilities and conduct an assessment of the Trustworthiness and Reliability (T&R) process and discussed the actions it plans to take to address them. Regarding these two recommendations, NRC plans to reevaluate these issues as part of its review of the effectiveness of the recently issued security regulations under 10 C.F.R. Part 37. This review is expected to occur 1 to 2 years after the regulations are implemented. According to NRC's comment letter, this review will serve as the basis for determining whether any additional security measures, guidance documents, rulemaking changes, or licensee outreach are appropriate. To that end, NRC stated in its technical comments that it independently evaluated the case we identified of an individual granted unescorted access, even though he had an extensive criminal history and had been convicted for terroristic threats. Based on its intial review, NRC noted that the event was an isolated incident and not a programmatic issue. However, without an assessment of the T&R process, which they have agreed to consider, NRC will not be able to determine the extent to which this case may represent a larger problem or if corrective actions are needed.

We recognize that a review of the effectiveness of the recently issued regulations will take time to complete. However, due to the serious nature of the security problems identified in our report, this reevaluation of the definition of collocation and the T&R process should be conducted by NRC with a greater sense of urgency. If NRC follows its current plan to address these recommendations in the time frame outlined in its comment letter, the review will not occur until 1 to 2 years after implentation of 10 C.F.R. Part 37. In the case of the 37 Agreement States, the earliest the review would occur is 1 to 2 years afer they issue their own compatible regulations—required by March 2016. The longer it takes for licensees to implement the security upgrades, the greater the risk that potentially dangerous radiological sources remain vulnerable and could be used as terrorist weapons.

As agreed with your offices, unless you publicly announce the contents of this report earlier, we plan no further distribution until 30 days from the report date. At that time, we will send copies of this report to the Administrator of NNSA, the Chairman of the Nuclear Regulatory Commission, the Secretary of Homeland Security, the appropriate congressional committees, and other interested parties. In addition, this report will be available at no charge on the GAO website at http://www.gao.gov.

If you or your staff members have any questions concerning this report, please contact me at (202) 512-3841 or trimbled@gao.gov. Contact points for our Offices of Congressional Relations and Public Affairs may be found on the last page of this report. GAO staff who made significant contributions to this report are listed in appendix IV.

David C. Trimble
Director, Natural Resources and Environment

Appendix I: Scope and Methodology

We focused our review primarily on the Nuclear Regulatory Commission (NRC) and the Department of Energy's (DOE) National Nuclear Security Administration (NNSA) because they are the principal federal agencies with responsibility for securing radiological material at industrial facilities in the United States. We also performed work at the Department of Homeland Security (DHS) because they are also involved in securing radiological sources, and we interviewed officials with responsibility for radiological security at the Department of Transportation (DOT) and United States Department of Agriculture (USDA). In addition, we interviewed an expert in the field of nuclear security, representatives from state government, and safety and security personnel at U.S. industrial facilities to discuss their views on how radiological sources are secured.

We visited 33 industrial facilities in California, Colorado, Hawaii, Pennsylvania, Texas, and Wyoming. These facilities included 15 industrial radiography companies, 6 commercial or sterilization companies, 5 academic research facilities, 3 well logging companies, 2 manufacturing and distribution companies, and 2 USDA facilities. The 33 facilities we visited are a nongeneralizable sample, selected on the basis of whether they were NRC states or Agreement States, the amount of curies contained in the devices using radiological sources, and the types of radiological devices. In addition, we considered if the site had undergone security upgrades funded by NNSA, and whether the site is located in a large urban area. At each location, we interviewed facility staff responsible for implementing procedures to secure the radiological sources, including questions about the use of security measures and if the licensee had made contact with NNSA. We also met with security personnel at sites, when available, and spoke to officials at some local law enforcement agencies responsible for security breaches.

We used NNSA's G-2 database, which aggregates data from NRC's National Source Tracking System (NSTS), to identify the location of industrial radiological sources, determine the different types of industrial devices that use radiological sources, and quantify curie amounts for different types of radiological sources. The G-2 data is based on information extracted from the NRC's 2011 NSTS database, the NRC's 2008 Sealed Source Inventory, and NNSA project team visits. G-2 contains all buildings in the United States that have risk-significant radiological sources (> 10 curies). To determine the reliability of these data, we conducted electronic testing and interviewed staff at NNSA and NRC about the reliability of these data. We tested these data to ensure their completeness and accuracy, and we determined that these data were sufficiently reliable to use in selecting locations to visit and summarizing the total number of facilities and the total number of curies.

To evaluate the challenges industrial licensees with industrial radiological sources face in securing these sources, we reviewed laws, regulations, and guidance related to the security of industrial radiological sources. We interviewed agency officials at NRC, NNSA, DHS, DOT, and USDA. We also interviewed state government officials in three states, and safety and security personnel at 33 industrial facilities we visited in six states, to obtain their views on how radiological sources are secured and what challenges they face in securing them. To identify thefts and incidents involving radiological sources, we reviewed relevant documentation and spoke to federal and state officials. We also spoke to officials at 33 industrial facilities we visited in California, Colorado, Hawaii, Pennsylvania, Texas, and Wyoming. At the facilities, we observed the security measures in place and spoke to officials in charge of implementing NRC and Agreement State security controls and overseeing the security measures.

To learn what steps federal agencies are taking to ensure radiological sources are secured at industrial facilities, we obtained information from and interviewed agency officials at NRC, NNSA, DOT, DHS, and USDA who are involved in securing sources and undertaking studies evaluating technologies related to source security. We also obtained information from Agreement States and NRC regions by reviewing documentation and interviewing officials at four Agreement States (California, Colorado, Texas, and Washington State) and one NRC regional office (Region IV) with responsibility for overseeing high-risk radiological sources. We selected these states and the NRC region based on the amount of curies and number of devices in the state containing radiological sources and the types of devices used. We also interviewed officials at DOE's Pacific Northwest National Laboratory about the status of efforts made to strengthen remote tracking of mobile devices containing radiological sources. We visited industrial facilities that received NNSA funded upgrades and security assessments in California, Hawaii, and Pennsylvania. To determine the costs of NNSA's security upgrades for industrial facilities, we obtained cost data from NNSA and interviewed the agency official who manages NNSA's Global Threat Reduction Initiative program. These data were used to determine the number of U.S. industrial facilities that have received NNSA security upgrades, as well as the total cost for completing these upgrades. We discussed the reliability of these data with knowledgeable NNSA officials and questioned them about the system's controls to verify the accuracy and completeness of the data. We also analyzed these data for missing information and obvious outliers. We found the data sufficiently reliable for our reporting purposes.

We conducted this performance audit from November 2012 to June 2014 in accordance with generally accepted government auditing standards. Those standards require that we plan and perform the audit to obtain sufficient, appropriate evidence to provide a reasonable basis for our findings and conclusions based on our audit objectives. We believe that the evidence obtained provides a reasonable basis for our findings and conclusions based on our audit objectives.

Department of Energy
National Nuclear Security Administration
Washington, DC 20585
May 22, 2014

Mr. David Trimble
Director
Natural Resources and Environment
Government Accountability Office
Washington, DC 20458

Dear Mr. Trimble:

Thank you for the opportunity to review the Government Accountability Office's (GAO) draft report titled, *Additional Actions Needed to Increase the Security of U.S. Industrial Radiological Sources,* (GAO-14-293). I understand the GAO began this review after the conclusion of its 2012 study on the security of radiological sources at U.S. medical facilities, redirecting focus to examine the challenges in reducing security risks posed by industrial radiological sources and the steps federal agencies are taking to improve security.

We agree challenges exist in reducing the security risks faced by U.S. licensees using high-risk industrial radiological sources. Specifically, licensees face challenges in securing mobile and stationary sources and protecting against an insider threat.

The GAO report makes three recommendations to the Nuclear Regulatory Commission (NRC), and one joint recommendation to NRC, the National Nuclear Security Administration (NNSA) and the Department of Homeland Security (DHS). NNSA is ready to support NRC efforts with technical expertise and other assistance as required in relation to the first three recommendations. The joint recommendation suggests the three agencies review existing collaboration mechanisms for enhancement opportunities, especially in the development and implementation of new technologies. NNSA concurs and will build on the current efforts to improve coordination with NRC, DHS and other relevant interagency partners to improve the security of radiological sources.

We appreciate the GAO's efforts and will use this information to pursue additional efforts with the specific goals of leveraging resources and expertise to improve the security of industrial radiological sources.

Printed with soy ink on recycled paper

If you have any questions regarding this response, please contact Dean Childs, Director, Office of Audit Coordination and Internal Affairs, at (301) 903-1341.

Sincerely,

Frank G. Klotz
Under Secretary for Nuclear Security
Administrator, NNSA

Enclosure

Appendix III: Comments from the Nuclear Regulatory Commission

UNITED STATES
NUCLEAR REGULATORY COMMISSION
WASHINGTON, D.C. 20555-0001

May 19, 2014

Glen Levis, Assistant, Director
Natural Resources and Environment
U.S. Government Accountability Office
Washington, DC 20548

Dear Mr. Levis:

Thank you for the opportunity to review and comment on the draft of your report GAO-14-293, "Additional Actions Needed to Increase the Security of U.S. Industrial Radiological Sources," which the Nuclear Regulatory Commission (NRC) received on April 24, 2014. The NRC appreciates the time and effort you and your staff have taken to review this topic.

Security and control of radioactive sources is a top priority for the NRC, which has a long history of ensuring radioactive source protection and security. In March 2013, the NRC issued a new rule, Title 10 of the *Code of Federal Regulations* (10 CFR) Part 37, "Physical Protection of Category 1 and Category 2 Quantities of Radioactive Material," which further enhanced security requirements for category 1 and 2 quantities of radioactive materials. The risk-informed and performance-based requirements of Part 37 represent a comprehensive, multi-layered program of security measures for radioactive materials that is focused on providing protection commensurate with the risk associated with the quantity of material possessed by the licensee.

Because the Part 37 regulations were not in effect at the time of the Government Accountability Office's (GAO) audit, the GAO report focused on the NRC security requirements that were issued to NRC licensees by order in accordance with the NRC's authority under the Atomic Energy Act of 1954, as amended. The new Part 37 rule did not simply codify the security orders, but expanded upon the security requirements in those orders. In drafting the Part 37 regulations, the NRC considered, among other things, the various orders issued, lessons learned during the implementation of the orders, experience obtained with voluntary security enhancements, and recommendations provided by and comments received from a wide variety of stakeholders. The resulting regulations provide a framework that requires licensees to develop security programs with measures specifically tailored to their facilities.

The NRC licensees were required to be in compliance with the new regulations by March 19, 2014, and Agreement States are currently in the process of implementing compatible requirements for their licensees, which must be completed by March 19, 2016. As stated below, the NRC is committed to reviewing the effectiveness of the requirements in 10 CFR Part 37 post-implementation to determine whether any additional enhancements are necessary. If additional measures are needed, the Commission will consider appropriate enhancements.

Enclosure 1 to this letter includes specific technical comments on the draft report and Enclosure 2 provides background information in support of one of our comments. The draft GAO report provided four recommendations, three of which recommend specific action by the

G. Levis   2

NRC. As discussed in Enclosure 2, NRC inspectors have already investigated and taken action on some of the GAO's concerns regarding the use of industrial sources. The NRC and the Agreement States will continue to pursue the examples in the report to ensure a complete understanding of the security concerns identified by the GAO and will incorporate any findings into the Part 37 effectiveness review.

Our comments on the recommendations are listed below:

• Recommendation: The NRC should obtain the views of key stakeholders, such as licensees, during the development of the Best Practices Guide to ensure that the guide contains the most relevant and useful information on securing the highest risk radiological sources.

  Response: The NRC agrees with the GAO's recommendation that the views of key stakeholders, such as licensees, should be obtained during the development of the guidance document, "Physical Security Best Practices for the Protection of Risk Significant Radioactive Material" (i.e., the Best Practices Guide). NRC and Agreement State inspectors interact with licensees during inspections to discuss questions and issues that the licensees have regarding the NRC's security requirements. The Best Practices Guide is being written to focus on areas of concern that licensees indicated to inspectors during the inspection process. In addition, the Department of Energy's National Nuclear Security Administration (NNSA) Global Threat Reduction Initiative, which is performing voluntary security upgrades and regularly interacts with NRC and Agreement State licensees, participated in the development of this Best Practices Guide.

  To address the concern raised by GAO in your report GAO-12-925, "Nuclear Nonproliferation: Additional Actions Needed to Improve Security of Radiological Sources at U.S. Medical Facilities," regarding improving the licensee's knowledge of acceptable security practices, the NRC is committed to publishing the Best Practices Guide in May 2014. However, during the first one to two years post implementation of 10 CFR Part 37, the NRC will assess the effectiveness of this guidance document to determine if any revisions to this document are needed, and will make revisions accordingly using our public participation process.

• Recommendation: The NRC should reconsider whether the definition of collocation should be revised for well logging facilities that routinely keep radiological sources in a single storage area but secured in separate storage containers.

  Response: The NRC acknowledges the GAO's recommendation that the definition of collocation should be reevaluated for well logging facilities that routinely keep radiological sources in a single storage area but secured in separate containers. During the first one to two year post-implementation period of 10 CFR Part 37, the NRC plans to conduct a preliminary review of the effectiveness of the requirements to determine whether any additional security measures, guidance documents (including revising NUREG-2155, "Implementation Guidance for 10 CFR Part 37 Physical Protection of Category 1 and 2 Quantities of Material" and the Best Practices Guide), rulemaking changes or licensee outreach are appropriate. The reevaluation of the definition of collocation will be included in this effort.

G. Levis   3

- Recommendation: The NRC should conduct an assessment of the Trustworthiness and
  Reliability (T&R) process to determine if it provides reasonable assurance against insider
  threat.

  Response: The NRC acknowledges the GAO's recommended assessment of the T&R
  process to determine if it provides reasonable assurance against an insider threat. As
  stated earlier, the NRC plans to conduct a preliminary review of the effectiveness of the
  10 CFR Part 37 requirements to determine whether any additional security measures,
  guidance documents, rulemaking changes or licensee outreach are appropriate. The
  reevaluation of the T&R process will be conducted as part of this effort.

- Recommendation: The Administrator of the National Nuclear Security Administration, the
  Chairman of the NRC, and the Secretary of the Department Homeland Security should
  review their existing collaboration mechanism for opportunities to enhance collaboration,
  especially in the development and implementation of new technologies.

  Response: The NRC agrees with this recommendation and will continue to conduct
  periodic meetings with senior management of these agencies to enhance coordination
  and collaboration on overarching technical and policy issues related to source security.
  As the GAO is aware, the NRC routinely collaborates with these agencies on a range of
  topics including the security of radiation sources. Both the NNSA and the Department of
  Homeland Security actively participate along with other agencies and State
  representatives on the Radiation Source Protection and Security Task Force, which is
  chaired by the Chairman of the NRC, consistent with the Energy Policy Act of 2005.

The NRC appreciates the opportunity to comment and to provide information about agency
actions being taken regarding the recommendations in the draft GAO report. Should you have
any questions, please contact Mr. Jesse Arildsen at (301) 415-1785.

Sincerely,

Michael F. Weber

for Mark A. Satorius
Executive Director
for Operations

Enclosures:
1. NRC Comments on GAO Draft Report
   GAO-14-293
2. Background Information

cc: David Trimble, GAO
    Jeffrey Barron, GAO

Appendix IV: GAO Contact and Staff Acknowledgments

GAO Contact	David C. Trimble, (202) 512-3841 or trimbled@gao.gov
Acknowledgments	In addition to the individual named above, Glen Levis (Assistant Director); Jeffrey Barron; Elizabeth Beardsley; Randy Cole; John Delicath; James Espinoza; Karen Keegan; Rebecca Shea; and Kiki Theodoropoulos made key contributions to this report.

www.ingramcontent.com/pod-product-compliance
Lightning Source LLC
Chambersburg PA
CBHW080550290526
45790CB00006B/2619